D1622363

This book is dedicated to my husband, Shanon,
who is my better half and reminds me that
part of time management is to remember
to live in the moment and that I don't have to
be efficient every hour of every day.
You complete me.

This book is also dedicated to you, dear reader.
The world needs you and the mark
you're going to make.
You are special, precious, and unique.
I can't wait to see you shine!

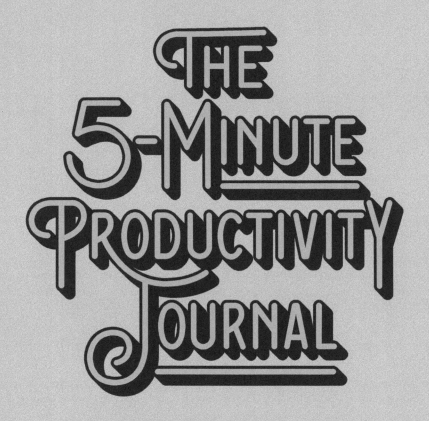

THE 5-Minute PRODUCTIVITY Journal

LITTLE CHALLENGES TO SPARK
MOTIVATION & EMPOWER YOU

Jennifer Webb

Illustrations by Lauren Griffin

ROCKRIDGE
PRESS

Copyright © 2020 by Rockridge Press, Emeryville, California

No part of this publication may be reproduced, stored in a retrieval system, or transmitted in any form or by any means, electronic, mechanical, photocopying, recording, scanning, or otherwise, except as permitted under Sections 107 or 108 of the 1976 United States Copyright Act, without the prior written permission of the Publisher. Requests to the Publisher for permission should be addressed to the Permissions Department, Rockridge Press, 6005 Shellmound Street, Suite 175, Emeryville, CA 94608.

Limit of Liability/Disclaimer of Warranty: The Publisher and the author make no representations or warranties with respect to the accuracy or completeness of the contents of this work and specifically disclaim all warranties, including without limitation warranties of fitness for a particular purpose. No warranty may be created or extended by sales or promotional materials. The advice and strategies contained herein may not be suitable for every situation. This work is sold with the understanding that the Publisher is not engaged in rendering medical, legal, or other professional advice or services. If professional assistance is required, the services of a competent professional person should be sought. Neither the Publisher nor the author shall be liable for damages arising herefrom. The fact that an individual, organization, or website is referred to in this work as a citation and/or potential source of further information does not mean that the author or the Publisher endorses the information the individual, organization, or website may provide or recommendations they/it may make. Further, readers should be aware that websites listed in this work may have changed or disappeared between when this work was written and when it is read.

For general information on our other products and services or to obtain technical support, please contact our Customer Care Department within the United States at (866) 744-2665, or outside the United States at (510) 253-0500.

Rockridge Press publishes its books in a variety of electronic and print formats. Some content that appears in print may not be available in electronic books, and vice versa.

TRADEMARKS: Rockridge Press and the Rockridge Press logo are trademarks or registered trademarks of Callisto Media Inc. and/or its affiliates, in the United States and other countries, and may not be used without written permission. All other trademarks are the property of their respective owners. Rockridge Press is not associated with any product or vendor mentioned in this book.

Interior and Cover Designer: Jill Lee

Art Producer: Samantha Ulban

Editor: Natasha Yglesias

Illustrations © 2020 Lauren Griffin.

Author photo courtesy of Christine Walker.

ISBN: Print 978-1-64739-854-5 | eBook 978-1-64739-855-2

R0

TABLE OF CONTENTS

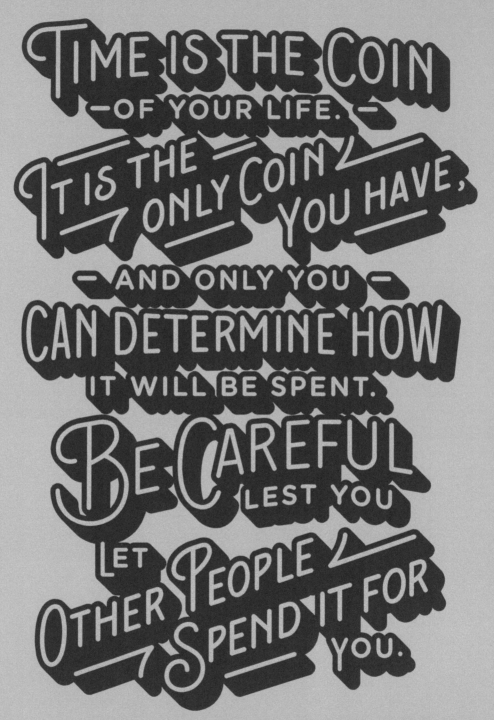

Time is the Coin of your life. It is the only coin you have, and only you can determine how it will be spent. Be careful lest you let other people spend it for you.

- CARL SANDBURG

THIS JOURNAL BELONGS TO:

INTRODUCTION

Time is a limited commodity. You have one life to live and a limited time to make an impact on the world, chase your dreams, and achieve your goals.

If you picked up this journal, you're most likely a passionate soul who wants to live in a deliberate way without wasting time. We have a choice on how to spend our time each day. This journal can help you use your time in a productive manner so that you can both chase (and catch) your dreams as well as have time to savor the journey along the way.

Like you, I fill many roles and have to manage my time effectively. I'm an author, personal development blogger, online course creator, mom, wife, friend, and much more. I strive to find a work/life balance and do so by defining my core values and priorities. I have to remind myself that I can do anything, but not everything.

When I wrote my book *Self-Discipline in 6 Weeks*, I went nuts on the time management chapter. To feel in control of your life, time management is one of the first things you have to learn. When you have an effective plan in place, you'll find yourself ahead of the game with time to spare. In short: Planning saves a great deal of time.

This journal will help you sort through the tangle of your to-do list and help you plan the most effective way to use your time. This way, you can focus your efforts on the pursuits that will give you the most reward. There are only so many hours in a day. Odds are, you're already working hard. What you need now is a way to work smarter. This journal is one way to accomplish that.

Designed to hone your focus, this journal is informed by research from neuroscience, positive psychology, and mindfulness practice, and based on new insights into motivation, habit formation, and resilience. I encourage you to use the initial Life Wheel and Goal Setting exercises before you dive into your journal entries. That way, you'll be able to go into each day lifted up, aware of how you're feeling and what needs to be done.

Think of time management as the key that unlocks other areas of your life. When you manage it wisely, you not only have time for your work, professional life, and family, you also find (or make) time for your creative widow.

Nothing in life is given to us. We can make goals all day long, but it takes work to achieve them. At the start of it all is prioritizing our tasks and taking our time by the horns. You're in charge of your life, your choices, and your time. What are you going to make happen today?

PART ONE

Your Best Life Starts Here

Empowering yourself to live your best life starts with good habits. When a behavior becomes a habit, you cease to actively think about it and do it on autopilot. Developing new positive habits requires some thought and time investment. This journal can help you put those new positive habits in place.

This journal will empower you to focus on what truly matters and make your day count. All it takes is five minutes a day to organize your thoughts, check in with how you're doing, and align your actions with your priorities.

GETTING STARTED

Using the Life Wheel and Goal Setting exercises, the journal will help you determine meaningful goals inspired by your authentic values. Then, by regularly completing journal entries, daily or a few times each week, you'll build a habit of focusing on what matters and staying in action on your goals. Whatever your desires and goals, be patient and compassionate with yourself.

To help identify your starting place, examine this list of habits and see which ones you're already doing and which ones you could add to your routines. Feel free to tweak them so they work best for you.

1. **Set SMART goals.**

   - SMART stands for specific, measurable, attainable, relevant, and timely. Much of our success with goals lies in how we structure them and how we hold ourselves accountable. The SMART goal structure sets you up for success because it helps break down large goals into logical, achievable chunks that can be completed within a specified time frame.

2. **Find a morning routine that works for you.**

   - A morning routine can help make you more productive the rest of the day. You might hit the ground running, or you might need some quiet time. Do what works best for you. When you find an option that feels right, keep doing it until it becomes a habit.

3. **Tackle your biggest task first thing in the morning.**

   - Morning is the most productive time of day for most people. If you have a task you find yourself dreading, or if the task is the biggest one on your to-do list—that's what you should prioritize. Tackle it first thing in the morning to maximize productivity.

4. Plan and prioritize.

- You probably have more on your to-do list than you can reasonably get done in a day. That's where planning comes in. When you plan ahead and prioritize, you go into your day knowing what you're going to do and when. This saves valuable time that's usually lost in regrouping and trying to decide on next steps.

5. Reflect and evaluate your goals.

- Sometimes we get so busy setting goals that we forget to pause and reflect to make sure those goals are still aligned with what we want. Goals aren't designed to be rigid, and they're not set in stone. They can be tweaked and tailored to help you reach your overall purpose at any time. If you never stop to evaluate and reflect, how will you know if your goals are really working to propel you forward?

6. Schedule "white space" into your day.

- White space is exactly what it sounds like—a blank area. In a picture, white space serves an important role: It draws the eye to focus on what's colored in. Without white space, the image becomes too "busy" and it's hard to focus on the main picture. When we fill our lives with constant business, it does the same. We find ourselves running and flitting from one thing to the next until we're exhausted. In that state, we can't focus on any one thing. Take the time to recharge. Leisure activities and rest will help you focus better.
- You aren't a machine. You can't be constantly efficient. Plan some downtime in your day just for you. Relax, spend time with your family, engage in healthy and creative hobbies that bring you happiness and peace. This "white space" in your day will allow you to recharge your batteries.

LIFE WHEEL EXERCISE

We all have multifaceted lives. Living well generally means bringing some sort of balance and fulfillment in each of those areas of our lives. Using time productively starts with understanding what really matters to you. It calls for taking a moment to reflect on how you feel about various aspects of your life. That's where the Life Wheel Exercise comes in.

Example Life Wheel

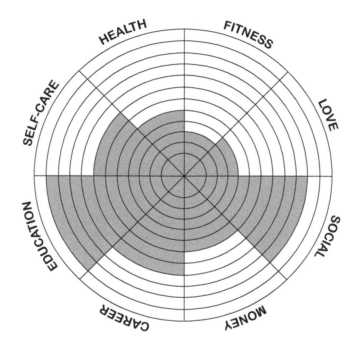

Fill in the life wheel by identifying eight or more areas of your life that are meaningful to you. Color the bars in the open version of the life wheel in each section to indicate how satisfied you are with each area of your life. Your areas don't have to be the same as in the example.

You'll find a blank life wheel after every 25 or so journal entries. This will help you see progress in each area as you use this journal. Part of an effective goal strategy is stopping to evaluate your goals to see if they're working for you or not. This life wheel is a powerful tool for you to do just that.

The blank life wheels will be blank circle graphs only, allowing you to customize them to best fit your needs.

Instructions for Creating Your Own Wheel

For your life wheel, choose themes that feel the most meaningful to you right now. You can split the wedges and add more themes if you need to, depending on how specific you want to be. Likewise, you can also have fewer wedges. Your life wheel is totally customizable.

If you need some ideas to get started, here are some example themes. Feel free to use any, all, or none of them.

- Health
- Fitness
- Love/romance
- Money
- Kids
- Extended family
- Career
- Social
- Education
- Friendships
- Hobbies
- Self-care
- Meditation
- Spiritual growth
- Home care
- Leisure time
- Adventures
- New skills
- Environment
- Creativity
- Community
- Mental health

Don't be discouraged if your satisfaction levels in your first life wheel aren't where you want them to be. Balance doesn't look the same for everyone. Remember you can do anything, but not *everything* (especially not at the same time).

It's perfectly normal for the satisfaction levels in your life wheel to go up and down. Much of it depends on where you're currently concentrating your efforts. The goal is not to have everything perfectly even, but to have all the themes at a place you're satisfied with at the present time. No one keeps perfect balance all the time.

The life wheel is here to help find gaps so you can fill them in and monitor areas of your life that still need work. We all juggle multiple things in our lives. When you concentrate time and effort in one area, it goes up, but inevitably other areas fall in the juggling act. That's okay. What the life wheel tells you is which things have fallen (or are falling) so you know where to pick them back up when you can.

Complete Your Life Wheel

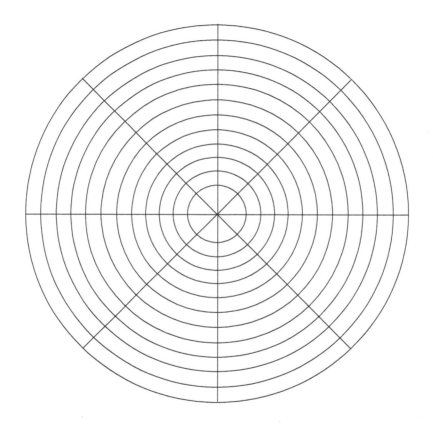

READY, SET, GOALS

Let's start goal setting. The first part of goal setting is understanding your values and priorities. Then you can go forward with confidence in pursuing your goals. To best understand your values and priorities, let's take self-inquiry a step deeper in order to pinpoint some meaningful goals.

1. What does productivity mean to you?

2. Write down the five things most important to you, in order of importance. For example, my top five ranking includes Serving God, Marriage, Family, Health, and Career.

3. Now that you've completed your life wheel, you might have deeper insights into how you feel about your current life circumstances. What sections of your life do you think you need to work on? Pick one to focus on first, and make sure it follows the SMART goal format: specific, measurable, attainable, relevant, and timely.

4. In order to stay true to ourselves, we must operate within the scope of our values. For example, two of my values are honesty and authenticity. Knowing your core values helps you set personal and professional boundaries and can help solidify your goals. List your core values below:

5. Where are you going? If you continue down the path you're on, where will you wind up? Is this where you want to be?

6. What do you really want? This is the last of the three magic questions from *Self-Discipline in 6 Weeks*. The answer is what I refer to as your "Big Why." This will be the reason and drive behind the goals you'll set. It'll fuel your motivation and keep you going forward when you want to quit. So, what do you want?

7. What are some of the challenges you face?

8. What are your strengths?

9. What's one habit you'll keep?

10. What's one habit you'll chuck?

PART TWO

The Journal Entries

Date: _____ Time: _____ Location: _____

I feel: _____

Why I feel this way: _____

_____

How'd it go yesterday? _____

_____

Yesterday's productivity: _____

Today's follow-through: _____

_____

Yesterday's act of self-care: _____

_____

What would make today great? _____

_____

I'm grateful for: _____

My top priority today: _____

What I'll do to support my top priority: _____

    ❑ **Step 1:** _____

    ❑ **Step 2:** _____

    ❑ **Step 3:** _____

Workday stopping time: _____

YOUR LITTLE CHALLENGE:

SAY "HELLO" TO A STRANGER TODAY.

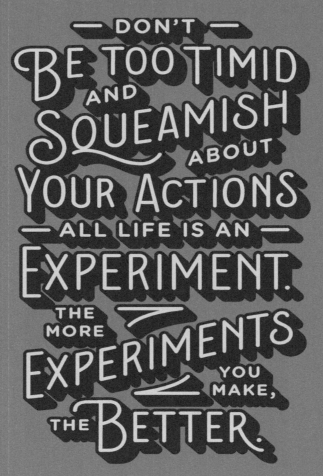

DON'T BE TOO TIMID AND SQUEAMISH ABOUT YOUR ACTIONS ALL LIFE IS AN EXPERIMENT. THE MORE EXPERIMENTS YOU MAKE, THE BETTER.

- RALPH WALDO EMERSON

Vent/Rejoice/Plan/Note/List:

Date: _____ Time: _____ Location: _____

I feel: _____

Why I feel this way: _____

_____

_____

How'd it go yesterday? _____

_____

_____

Yesterday's productivity: _____

Today's follow-through: _____

_____

_____

Yesterday's act of self-care: _____

_____

_____

What would make today great? _____

_____

_____

I'm grateful for: _____

My top priority today: _____

What I'll do to support my top priority: _____

    ❑ **Step 1:** _____

    ❑ **Step 2:** _____

    ❑ **Step 3:** _____

Workday stopping time: _____

Vent/Rejoice/Plan/Note/List:

YOUR LITTLE CHALLENGE:

CLEAR THE AIR WITH SOMEONE YOU'VE HAD AN AWKWARD MOMENT WITH LATELY.

Date: _____ Time: _____ Location: _____

I feel: _____

Why I feel this way: _____

_____

_____

How'd it go yesterday? _____

_____

_____

Yesterday's productivity: _____

Today's follow-through: _____

_____

_____

Yesterday's act of self-care: _____

_____

_____

What would make today great? _____

_____

_____

I'm grateful for: _____

My top priority today: _____

What I'll do to support my top priority: _____

     ❑ **Step 1:** _____

     ❑ **Step 2:** _____

     ❑ **Step 3:** _____

Workday stopping time: _____

Vent/Rejoice/Plan/Note/List:

WRITE DOWN YOUR PROUDEST MOMENT
OF THE PAST 24 HOURS

Date: _____ Time: _____ Location: _____

I feel: _____

Why I feel this way: _____

_____

_____

How'd it go yesterday? _____

_____

_____

Yesterday's productivity: _____

Today's follow-through: _____

_____

_____

Yesterday's act of self-care: _____

_____

_____

What would make today great? _____

_____

_____

I'm grateful for: _____

My top priority today: _____

What I'll do to support my top priority: _____

    ❑ **Step 1:** _____

    ❑ **Step 2:** _____

    ❑ **Step 3:** _____

Workday stopping time: _____

Vent/Rejoice/Plan/Note/List:

_____

_____

_____

_____

_____

_____

_____

_____

_____

_____

_____

_____

_____

_____

_____

_____

YOUR LITTLE CHALLENGE:

BLOCK OFF ONE HOUR THIS WEEK AND PLAN NOTHING UNTIL THAT HOUR BEGINS.

Date: _____ Time: _____ Location: _____

I feel: _____

Why I feel this way: _____

_____

_____

How'd it go yesterday? _____

_____

_____

Yesterday's productivity: _____

Today's follow-through: _____

_____

_____

Yesterday's act of self-care: _____

_____

_____

What would make today great? _____

_____

_____

I'm grateful for: _____

My top priority today: _____

What I'll do to support my top priority: _____

    ❑ **Step 1:** _____

    ❑ **Step 2:** _____

    ❑ **Step 3:** _____

Workday stopping time: _____

Vent/Rejoice/Plan/Note/List:

YOUR LITTLE CHALLENGE:

EAT AT A RESTAURANT YOU'VE ALWAYS WANTED TO TRY.
MAYBE ORDER A DISH YOU WOULDN'T USUALLY GET.

Date: _____ Time: _____ Location: _____

I feel: _____

Why I feel this way: _____

_____

How'd it go yesterday? _____

_____

Yesterday's productivity: _____

Today's follow-through: _____

_____

Yesterday's act of self-care: _____

_____

What would make today great? _____

_____

I'm grateful for: _____

My top priority today: _____

What I'll do to support my top priority: _____

    ❏ **Step 1:** _____

    ❏ **Step 2:** _____

    ❏ **Step 3:** _____

Workday stopping time: _____

YOUR LITTLE CHALLENGE:

SAY "HELLO" TO A STRANGER TODAY.

NEVER GIVE UP, FOR THAT IS JUST THE PLACE AND TIME — THE — TIDE WILL TURN.

- OLDTOWN FOLKS,
HARRIET BEECHER STOWE

Vent/Rejoice/Plan/Note/List:

Date: _____ Time: _____ Location: _____

I feel: _____

Why I feel this way: _____

_____

_____

How'd it go yesterday? _____

_____

_____

Yesterday's productivity: _____

Today's follow-through: _____

_____

_____

Yesterday's act of self-care: _____

_____

_____

What would make today great? _____

_____

_____

I'm grateful for: _____

My top priority today: _____

What I'll do to support my top priority: _____

- ❑ **Step 1:** _____
- ❑ **Step 2:** _____
- ❑ **Step 3:** _____

Workday stopping time: _____

Vent/Rejoice/Plan/Note/List:

YOUR LITTLE CHALLENGE:

WHEN DID YOU SEE YOUR STRENGTH TODAY?

Date: _____ Time: _____ Location: _____

I feel: _____

Why I feel this way: _____

_____

_____

How'd it go yesterday? _____

_____

_____

Yesterday's productivity: _____

Today's follow-through: _____

_____

_____

Yesterday's act of self-care: _____

_____

_____

What would make today great? _____

_____

_____

I'm grateful for: _____

My top priority today: _____

What I'll do to support my top priority: _____

    ❑ **Step 1:** _____

    ❑ **Step 2:** _____

    ❑ **Step 3:** _____

Workday stopping time: _____

Vent/Rejoice/Plan/Note/List:

_____

_____

_____

_____

_____

_____

_____

_____

_____

_____

_____

_____

_____

_____

_____

_____

_____

_____

_____

YOUR LITTLE CHALLENGE:

GO FOR A 15-MINUTE WALK OUTSIDE. PAY ATTENTION TO THE SOUNDS AROUND YOU, THE FEEL OF THE BREEZE ON YOUR FACE, AND THE GROUND BENEATH YOUR FEET.

Date: _____ Time: _____ Location: _____

I feel: _____

Why I feel this way: _____

_____

_____

How'd it go yesterday? _____

_____

_____

Yesterday's productivity: _____

Today's follow-through: _____

_____

_____

Yesterday's act of self-care: _____

_____

_____

What would make today great? _____

_____

_____

I'm grateful for: _____

My top priority today: _____

What I'll do to support my top priority: _____

    ❑ **Step 1:** _____

    ❑ **Step 2:** _____

    ❑ **Step 3:** _____

Workday stopping time: _____

Vent/Rejoice/Plan/Note/List:

_____

_____

_____

_____

_____

_____

_____

_____

_____

_____

_____

_____

_____

_____

_____

YOUR LITTLE CHALLENGE:

TRAVEL A DIFFERENT WAY HOME FROM WORK.
TAKE IN YOUR NEW SURROUNDINGS.

Date: _____ Time: _____ Location: _____

I feel: _____

Why I feel this way: _____

_____

_____

How'd it go yesterday? _____

_____

_____

Yesterday's productivity: _____

Today's follow-through: _____

_____

_____

Yesterday's act of self-care: _____

_____

_____

What would make today great? _____

_____

_____

I'm grateful for: _____

My top priority today: _____

What I'll do to support my top priority: _____

- ❑ **Step 1:** _____

- ❑ **Step 2:** _____

- ❑ **Step 3:** _____

Workday stopping time: _____

Vent/Rejoice/Plan/Note/List:

_____

_____

_____

_____

_____

_____

_____

_____

_____

_____

_____

_____

_____

_____

_____

_____

_____

_____

_____

_____

YOUR LITTLE CHALLENGE:

"GENIUS IS ONE PERCENT INSPIRATION AND NINETY-NINE PERCENT PERSPIRATION". -THOMAS EDISON WRITE DOWN HOW THIS QUOTE IS TRUE FOR YOU.

Date: _____ Time: _____ Location: _____

I feel: _____

Why I feel this way: _____

_____

How'd it go yesterday? _____

_____

Yesterday's productivity: _____

Today's follow-through: _____

_____

Yesterday's act of self-care: _____

_____

What would make today great? _____

_____

I'm grateful for: _____

My top priority today: _____

What I'll do to support my top priority: _____

    ❑ **Step 1:** _____

    ❑ **Step 2:** _____

    ❑ **Step 3:** _____

Workday stopping time: _____

YOUR LITTLE CHALLENGE:

LOOK IN THE MIRROR AND GIVE YOURSELF A PEP TALK.

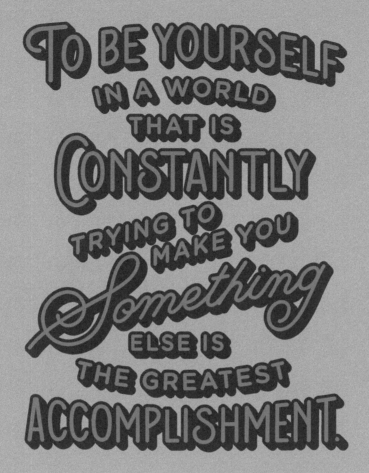

TO BE YOURSELF IN A WORLD THAT IS CONSTANTLY TRYING TO MAKE YOU Something ELSE IS THE GREATEST ACCOMPLISHMENT.

- RALPH WALDO EMERSON

Vent/Rejoice/Plan/Note/List:

Date: _____ Time: _____ Location: _____

I feel: _____

Why I feel this way: _____

_____

_____

How'd it go yesterday? _____

_____

_____

Yesterday's productivity: _____

Today's follow-through: _____

_____

_____

Yesterday's act of self-care: _____

_____

_____

What would make today great? _____

_____

_____

I'm grateful for: _____

My top priority today: _____

What I'll do to support my top priority: _____

    ❑ **Step 1:** _____

    ❑ **Step 2:** _____

    ❑ **Step 3:** _____

Workday stopping time: _____

Vent/Rejoice/Plan/Note/List:

_____

_____

_____

_____

_____

_____

_____

_____

_____

_____

_____

_____

_____

_____

_____

_____

_____

_____

_____

_____

YOUR LITTLE CHALLENGE:

REACH OUT TO A FRIEND YOU'VE BEEN MEANING TO CHECK IN WITH. INVITE THEM FOR A COFFEE.

Date: _____ Time: _____ Location: _____

I feel: _____

Why I feel this way: _____

_____

_____

How'd it go yesterday? _____

_____

_____

Yesterday's productivity: _____

Today's follow-through: _____

_____

_____

Yesterday's act of self-care: _____

_____

_____

What would make today great? _____

_____

_____

I'm grateful for: _____

My top priority today: _____

What I'll do to support my top priority: _____

    ❏ **Step 1:** _____

    ❏ **Step 2:** _____

    ❏ **Step 3:** _____

Workday stopping time: _____

Vent/Rejoice/Plan/Note/List:

YOUR LITTLE CHALLENGE:

FIND A RECIPE THAT'S DIFFERENT FROM YOUR NORM.
COOK, EAT, AND (HOPEFULLY) ENJOY!
(THE WORST THAT CAN HAPPEN IS HAVING TO ORDER
PIZZA, RIGHT?)

Date: _____ Time: _____ Location: _____

I feel: _____

Why I feel this way: _____

_____

_____

How'd it go yesterday? _____

_____

_____

Yesterday's productivity: _____

Today's follow-through: _____

_____

_____

Yesterday's act of self-care: _____

_____

_____

What would make today great? _____

_____

_____

I'm grateful for: _____

My top priority today: _____

What I'll do to support my top priority: _____

    ❑ **Step 1:** _____

    ❑ **Step 2:** _____

    ❑ **Step 3:** _____

Workday stopping time: _____

Vent/Rejoice/Plan/Note/List:

YOUR LITTLE CHALLENGE:

IDENTIFY ONE PROJECT YOU'VE DONE IN THE PAST THAT YOU COULD DO BETTER NOW. HOW WOULD YOU IMPROVE IT?

Date: _____ Time: _____ Location: _____

I feel: _____

Why I feel this way: _____

_____

_____

How'd it go yesterday? _____

_____

_____

Yesterday's productivity: _____

Today's follow-through: _____

_____

_____

Yesterday's act of self-care: _____

_____

_____

What would make today great? _____

_____

_____

I'm grateful for: _____

My top priority today: _____

What I'll do to support my top priority: _____

❏ **Step 1:** _____

❏ **Step 2:** _____

❏ **Step 3:** _____

Workday stopping time: _____

Vent/Rejoice/Plan/Note/List:

YOUR LITTLE CHALLENGE:

WRITE DOWN FIVE CHARACTERISTICS YOU LIKE ABOUT YOURSELF.

Date: _____ Time: _____ Location: _____

I feel: _____

Why I feel this way: _____

_____

How'd it go yesterday? _____

_____

Yesterday's productivity: _____

Today's follow-through: _____

_____

Yesterday's act of self-care: _____

_____

What would make today great? _____

_____

I'm grateful for: _____

My top priority today: _____

What I'll do to support my top priority: _____

❑ **Step 1:** _____

❑ **Step 2:** _____

❑ **Step 3:** _____

Workday stopping time: _____

YOUR LITTLE CHALLENGE:

BLOCK OUT AN HOUR THIS WEEKEND TO DO A HOBBY YOU LOVE.

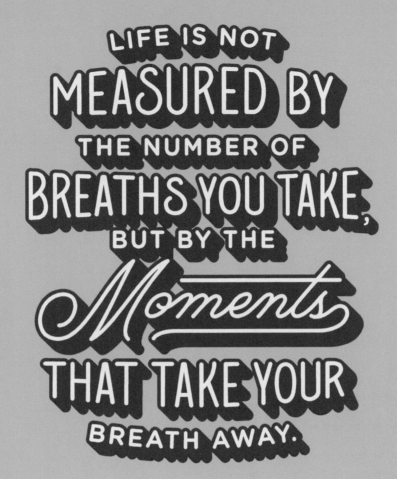

LIFE IS NOT MEASURED BY THE NUMBER OF BREATHS YOU TAKE, BUT BY THE *Moments* THAT TAKE YOUR BREATH AWAY.

- MAYA ANGELOU

Vent/Rejoice/Plan/Note/List:

Date: _____ Time: _____ Location: _____

I feel: _____

Why I feel this way: _____

_____

How'd it go yesterday? _____

_____

Yesterday's productivity: _____

Today's follow-through: _____

_____

Yesterday's act of self-care: _____

_____

What would make today great? _____

_____

I'm grateful for: _____

My top priority today: _____

What I'll do to support my top priority: _____

    ❑ **Step 1:** _____

    ❑ **Step 2:** _____

    ❑ **Step 3:** _____

Workday stopping time: _____

YOUR LITTLE CHALLENGE:

INTRODUCE YOURSELF TO SOMEONE YOU ADMIRE. TELL THEM WHY YOU ADMIRE THEM.

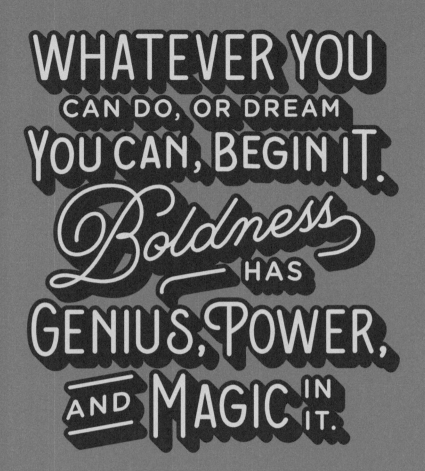

WHATEVER YOU CAN DO, OR DREAM YOU CAN, BEGIN IT. Boldness HAS GENIUS, POWER, AND MAGIC IN IT.

- UNKNOWN

Vent/Rejoice/Plan/Note/List:

Date: _____ Time: _____ Location: _____

I feel: _____

Why I feel this way: _____

_____

_____

How'd it go yesterday? _____

_____

_____

Yesterday's productivity: _____

Today's follow-through: _____

_____

_____

Yesterday's act of self-care: _____

_____

_____

What would make today great? _____

_____

_____

I'm grateful for: _____

My top priority today: _____

What I'll do to support my top priority: _____

    ❏ **Step 1:** _____

    ❏ **Step 2:** _____

    ❏ **Step 3:** _____

Workday stopping time: _____

Vent/Rejoice/Plan/Note/List:

_____

_____

_____

_____

_____

_____

_____

_____

_____

_____

_____

_____

_____

_____

_____

_____

_____

_____

_____

_____

YOUR LITTLE CHALLENGE:

SOMETHING IN YOUR LIFE NOT WORKING? BRAINSTORM A LIST OF OTHER POSSIBLE WAYS TO MAKE IT A SUCCESS.

Date: _____ Time: _____ Location: _____

I feel: _____

Why I feel this way: _____

_____

_____

How'd it go yesterday? _____

_____

_____

Yesterday's productivity: _____

Today's follow-through: _____

_____

_____

Yesterday's act of self-care: _____

_____

_____

What would make today great? _____

_____

_____

I'm grateful for: _____

My top priority today: _____

What I'll do to support my top priority: _____

❑ **Step 1:** _____

❑ **Step 2:** _____

❑ **Step 3:** _____

Workday stopping time: _____

Vent/Rejoice/Plan/Note/List:

YOUR LITTLE CHALLENGE:

WHAT'S ONE THING YOUR INNER CRITIC ALWAYS TELLS YOU? INVESTIGATE THE REAL MESSAGE THAT'S THERE. INNER CRITICS OFTEN TRY TO BE HELPFUL, THEY'RE JUST VERY BAD AT THEIR JOBS!

Date: _____ Time: _____ Location: _____

I feel: _____

Why I feel this way: _____

_____

_____

How'd it go yesterday? _____

_____

_____

Yesterday's productivity: _____

Today's follow-through: _____

_____

_____

Yesterday's act of self-care: _____

_____

_____

What would make today great? _____

_____

_____

I'm grateful for: _____

My top priority today: _____

What I'll do to support my top priority: _____

    ❑ **Step 1:** _____

    ❑ **Step 2:** _____

    ❑ **Step 3:** _____

Workday stopping time: _____

Vent/Rejoice/Plan/Note/List:

_____

_____

_____

_____

_____

_____

_____

_____

_____

_____

_____

_____

_____

_____

_____

_____

_____

_____

_____

_____

YOUR LITTLE CHALLENGE:

FIND A TIME YOU CAN BE ALONE AND UNDISTURBED FOR FIVE MINUTES. TRY TO CLEAR YOUR MIND. WHEN IT WANDERS, BRING IT BACK. EVALUATE HOW YOU DID AT THE END OF THE FIVE MINUTES.

Date: _____ Time: _____ Location: _____

I feel: _____

Why I feel this way: _____

_____

_____

How'd it go yesterday? _____

_____

_____

Yesterday's productivity: _____

Today's follow-through: _____

_____

_____

Yesterday's act of self-care: _____

_____

_____

What would make today great? _____

_____

_____

I'm grateful for: _____

My top priority today: _____

What I'll do to support my top priority: _____

    ❑ **Step 1:** _____

    ❑ **Step 2:** _____

    ❑ **Step 3:** _____

Workday stopping time: _____

Vent/Rejoice/Plan/Note/List:

_____

_____

_____

_____

_____

_____

_____

_____

_____

_____

_____

_____

_____

_____

_____

_____

YOUR LITTLE CHALLENGE:

CHECK OUT A BOOK FROM THE LIBRARY OR WATCH A
DOCUMENTARY ON SOMETHING YOU'VE ALWAYS
BEEN CURIOUS ABOUT.

Date: _____ Time: _____ Location: _____

I feel: _____

Why I feel this way: _____

_____

How'd it go yesterday? _____

_____

Yesterday's productivity: _____

Today's follow-through: _____

_____

Yesterday's act of self-care: _____

_____

What would make today great? _____

_____

I'm grateful for: _____

My top priority today: _____

What I'll do to support my top priority: _____

❑ **Step 1:** _____

❑ **Step 2:** _____

❑ **Step 3:** _____

Workday stopping time: _____

YOUR LITTLE CHALLENGE:

BE SUPPORTIVE TO ANOTHER PERSON TODAY.

THERE IS NO *Failure* — EXCEPT IN — NO LONGER *Trying.*

- ELBERT HUBBARD

Vent/Rejoice/Plan/Note/List:

Date: _____ Time: _____ Location: _____

I feel: _____

Why I feel this way: _____

_____

_____

How'd it go yesterday? _____

_____

_____

Yesterday's productivity: _____

Today's follow-through: _____

_____

_____

Yesterday's act of self-care: _____

_____

_____

What would make today great? _____

_____

_____

I'm grateful for: _____

My top priority today: _____

What I'll do to support my top priority: _____

    ❑ **Step 1:** _____

    ❑ **Step 2:** _____

    ❑ **Step 3:** _____

Workday stopping time: _____

Vent/Rejoice/Plan/Note/List:

IDENTIFY AN AREA OR INSTANCE WHERE YOU WERE TOO HARD ON YOURSELF. WHAT WOULD YOU HAVE SAID IF YOU WERE TALKING TO A FRIEND?

Date: _____ Time: _____ Location: _____

I feel: _____

Why I feel this way: _____

_____

_____

How'd it go yesterday? _____

_____

_____

Yesterday's productivity: _____

Today's follow-through: _____

_____

_____

Yesterday's act of self-care: _____

_____

_____

What would make today great? _____

_____

_____

I'm grateful for: _____

My top priority today: _____

What I'll do to support my top priority: _____

❑ **Step 1:** _____

❑ **Step 2:** _____

❑ **Step 3:** _____

Workday stopping time: _____

Vent/Rejoice/Plan/Note/List:

_____

_____

_____

_____

_____

_____

_____

_____

_____

_____

_____

_____

_____

_____

_____

_____

_____

_____

_____

YOUR LITTLE CHALLENGE:

RESET THE WALLPAPER ON YOUR PHONE TO IMAGES THAT MAKE YOU SMILE AND/OR RELAX YOU.

Date: _____ Time: _____ Location: _____

I feel: _____

Why I feel this way: _____

_____

_____

How'd it go yesterday? _____

_____

_____

Yesterday's productivity: _____

Today's follow-through: _____

_____

_____

Yesterday's act of self-care: _____

_____

_____

What would make today great? _____

_____

_____

I'm grateful for: _____

My top priority today: _____

What I'll do to support my top priority: _____

    ❏ **Step 1:** _____

    ❏ **Step 2:** _____

    ❏ **Step 3:** _____

Workday stopping time: _____

Vent/Rejoice/Plan/Note/List:

_____
_____
_____
_____
_____
_____
_____
_____
_____
_____
_____
_____
_____
_____
_____
_____
_____
_____
_____

YOUR LITTLE CHALLENGE:

KNOW SOMEONE IN YOUR COMPANY WHO ROCKS AT A JOB YOU WANT TO DO? OFFER TO BUY THEM LUNCH IN EXCHANGE FOR AN INFORMATIONAL INTERVIEW. SUCCESS LEAVES FOOTPRINTS THAT YOU CAN FOLLOW!

Update Your Life Wheel

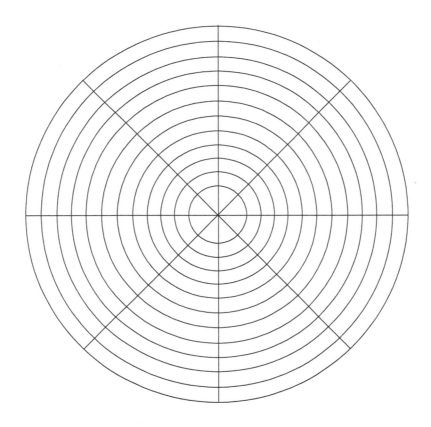

Date: _____ Time: _____ Location: _____

I feel: _____

Why I feel this way: _____

_____

_____

How'd it go yesterday? _____

_____

_____

Yesterday's productivity: _____

Today's follow-through: _____

_____

_____

Yesterday's act of self-care: _____

_____

_____

What would make today great? _____

_____

_____

I'm grateful for: _____

My top priority today: _____

What I'll do to support my top priority: _____

    ❑ **Step 1:** _____

    ❑ **Step 2:** _____

    ❑ **Step 3:** _____

Workday stopping time: _____

Vent/Rejoice/Plan/Note/List:

YOUR LITTLE CHALLENGE:

INDENTIFY AND WRITE DOWN AN UNDERLYING FEAR OR LIMITING BELIEF THAT'S HOLDING YOU BACK FROM GROWING. INVESTIGATE WHY IT'S THERE.

Date: _____ Time: _____ Location: _____

I feel: _____

Why I feel this way: _____

_____

How'd it go yesterday? _____

_____

Yesterday's productivity: _____

Today's follow-through: _____

_____

Yesterday's act of self-care: _____

_____

What would make today great? _____

_____

I'm grateful for: _____

My top priority today: _____

What I'll do to support my top priority: _____

❑ **Step 1:** _____

❑ **Step 2:** _____

❑ **Step 3:** _____

Workday stopping time: _____

YOUR LITTLE CHALLENGE:

WRITE AN ENCOURAGING LETTER TO YOURSELF. KEEP IT FOR A DAY WHEN YOU'RE FEELING DOWN AND READ IT THEN.

- MARK TWAIN

Vent/Rejoice/Plan/Note/List:

_____

_____

_____

_____

_____

_____

_____

Date: _____ Time: _____ Location: _____

I feel: _____

Why I feel this way: _____

_____

_____

How'd it go yesterday? _____

_____

_____

Yesterday's productivity: _____

Today's follow-through: _____

_____

_____

Yesterday's act of self-care: _____

_____

_____

What would make today great? _____

_____

_____

I'm grateful for: _____

My top priority today: _____

What I'll do to support my top priority: _____

    ❑ **Step 1:** _____

    ❑ **Step 2:** _____

    ❑ **Step 3:** _____

Workday stopping time: _____

Vent/Rejoice/Plan/Note/List:

YOUR LITTLE CHALLENGE:

TAKE YOURSELF ON AN IMAGINARY MINI-VACATION. CLOSE
YOUR EYES AND PICTURE A PLACE IN VIVID DETAIL. WHAT
CAN YOU HEAR, TASTE, SMELL? SEE IF YOU CAN ACHIEVE
ANY OF THESE SENSATIONS AT HOME.

Date: _____ Time: _____ Location: _____

I feel: _____

Why I feel this way: _____

_____

_____

How'd it go yesterday? _____

_____

_____

Yesterday's productivity: _____

Today's follow-through: _____

_____

_____

Yesterday's act of self-care: _____

_____

_____

What would make today great? _____

_____

_____

I'm grateful for: _____

My top priority today: _____

What I'll do to support my top priority: _____

    ❑ **Step 1:** _____

    ❑ **Step 2:** _____

    ❑ **Step 3:** _____

Workday stopping time: _____

Vent/Rejoice/Plan/Note/List:

_____

_____

_____

_____

_____

_____

_____

_____

_____

_____

_____

_____

_____

_____

_____

_____

_____

_____

_____

YOUR LITTLE CHALLENGE:

BRAINSTORM ABOUT WHAT'S HOLDING YOU BACK FROM ACHIEVING A GOAL. SEE IF THERE ARE SMALL STEPS YOU CAN TAKE TO CONFRONT WHAT'S STOPPING YOU.

Date: _____ Time: _____ Location: _____

I feel: _____

Why I feel this way: _____

_____

_____

How'd it go yesterday? _____

_____

_____

Yesterday's productivity: _____

Today's follow-through: _____

_____

_____

Yesterday's act of self-care: _____

_____

_____

What would make today great? _____

_____

_____

I'm grateful for: _____

My top priority today: _____

What I'll do to support my top priority: _____

❑ **Step 1:** _____

❑ **Step 2:** _____

❑ **Step 3:** _____

Workday stopping time: _____

Vent/Rejoice/Plan/Note/List:

YOUR LITTLE CHALLENGE:

WRITE DOWN AN INSPIRATIONAL QUOTE (OR FOR SOME, A BIBLE VERSE) THAT KEEPS YOU GOING WHEN YOU WANT TO QUIT. PUT IT SOMEWHERE YOU'LL SEE EVERY DAY.

Date: _____ Time: _____ Location: _____

I feel: _____

Why I feel this way: _____

_____

_____

How'd it go yesterday? _____

_____

_____

Yesterday's productivity: _____

Today's follow-through: _____

_____

_____

Yesterday's act of self-care: _____

_____

_____

What would make today great? _____

_____

_____

I'm grateful for: _____

My top priority today: _____

What I'll do to support my top priority: _____

❑ **Step 1:** _____

❑ **Step 2:** _____

❑ **Step 3:** _____

Workday stopping time: _____

Vent/Rejoice/Plan/Note/List:

YOUR LITTLE CHALLENGE:

THINK OF A PERSON YOU KNOW WHO'S SUPPORTIVE. WHEN YOU'VE HAD A ROUGH DAY, TALK TO YOURSELF WITH THE WORDS THAT PERSON WOULD USE.

Date: _____ Time: _____ Location: _____

I feel: _____

Why I feel this way: _____
_____

How'd it go yesterday? _____
_____

Yesterday's productivity: _____

Today's follow-through: _____
_____

Yesterday's act of self-care: _____
_____

What would make today great? _____
_____

I'm grateful for: _____

My top priority today: _____

What I'll do to support my top priority:

    ❏ **Step 1:** _____

    ❏ **Step 2:** _____

    ❏ **Step 3:** _____

Workday stopping time: _____

YOUR LITTLE CHALLENGE:

TAKE YOURSELF ON A DATE. TREAT YOURSELF!

BE HAPPY IN THE Moment, — THAT'S ENOUGH.— EACH MOMENT IS ALL WE NEED, NOT MORE.

- MOTHER TERESA

Vent/Rejoice/Plan/Note/List:

Date: _____ Time: _____ Location: _____

I feel: _____

Why I feel this way: _____

_____

How'd it go yesterday? _____

_____

Yesterday's productivity: _____

Today's follow-through: _____

_____

Yesterday's act of self-care: _____

_____

What would make today great? _____

_____

I'm grateful for: _____

My top priority today: _____

What I'll do to support my top priority: _____

    ❑ **Step 1:** _____

    ❑ **Step 2:** _____

    ❑ **Step 3:** _____

Workday stopping time: _____

YOUR LITTLE CHALLENGE:

TAKE A (SMALL) FASHION RISK TODAY.

THE BITTEREST TEARS SHED OVER GRAVES ARE FOR WORDS LEFT UNSAID AND DEEDS LEFT UNDONE.

- HARRIET BEECHER STOWE

Vent/Rejoice/Plan/Note/List:

Date: _____ Time: _____ Location: _____

I feel: _____

Why I feel this way: _____

_____

_____

How'd it go yesterday? _____

_____

_____

Yesterday's productivity: _____

Today's follow-through: _____

_____

_____

Yesterday's act of self-care: _____

_____

_____

What would make today great? _____

_____

_____

I'm grateful for: _____

My top priority today: _____

What I'll do to support my top priority: _____

    ❑ **Step 1:** _____

    ❑ **Step 2:** _____

    ❑ **Step 3:** _____

Workday stopping time: _____

Vent/Rejoice/Plan/Note/List:

YOUR LITTLE CHALLENGE:

IS THERE A POPULAR SHOW, MOVIE, OR BOOK THAT YOU
JUST COULDN'T GET INTO? TRY GIVING IT ANOTHER GO
AND SEE IF IT STICKS. IF NOT, AT LEAST YOU CAN SAY
YOU GAVE IT A FAIR SHOT.

Date: _____ Time: _____ Location: _____

I feel: _____

Why I feel this way: _____

_____

_____

How'd it go yesterday? _____

_____

_____

Yesterday's productivity: _____

Today's follow-through: _____

_____

_____

Yesterday's act of self-care: _____

_____

_____

What would make today great? _____

_____

_____

I'm grateful for: _____

My top priority today: _____

What I'll do to support my top priority: _____

❑ **Step 1:** _____

❑ **Step 2:** _____

❑ **Step 3:** _____

Workday stopping time: _____

Vent/Rejoice/Plan/Note/List:

YOUR LITTLE CHALLENGE:

FIND AN INSPIRATIONAL QUOTE OR BIBLE VERSE THAT REMINDS YOU TO BE KIND TO YOURSELF. REFER TO IT WHEN YOUR INNER CRITIC BECOMES TOO MUCH AND GIVE YOURSELF SOME LOVE.

The Journal Entries   81

Date: _____ Time: _____ Location: _____

I feel: _____

Why I feel this way: _____

_____

_____

How'd it go yesterday? _____

_____

_____

Yesterday's productivity: _____

Today's follow-through: _____

_____

_____

Yesterday's act of self-care: _____

_____

_____

What would make today great? _____

_____

_____

I'm grateful for: _____

My top priority today: _____

What I'll do to support my top priority: _____

□ **Step 1:** _____

□ **Step 2:** _____

□ **Step 3:** _____

Workday stopping time: _____

Vent/Rejoice/Plan/Note/List:

YOUR LITTLE CHALLENGE:

COOK YOURSELF A MEAL YOU LOVE. SAVOR EVERY BITE.

Date: _____ Time: _____ Location: _____

I feel: _____

Why I feel this way: _____

_____

How'd it go yesterday? _____

_____

Yesterday's productivity: _____

Today's follow-through: _____

_____

Yesterday's act of self-care: _____

_____

What would make today great? _____

_____

I'm grateful for: _____

My top priority today: _____

What I'll do to support my top priority: _____

    ❑ **Step 1:** _____

    ❑ **Step 2:** _____

    ❑ **Step 3:** _____

Workday stopping time: _____

Vent/Rejoice/Plan/Note/List:

YOUR LITTLE CHALLENGE:

VOLUNTEER AT A LOCAL ORGANIZATION FOR A DAY ANIMAL SHELTER, HOMELESSS SHELTER, LIBRARY, SCHOOL—WHATEVER EXCITES YOU MOST).

Date: _____ Time: _____ Location: _____

I feel: _____

Why I feel this way: _____

_____

How'd it go yesterday? _____

_____

Yesterday's productivity: _____

Today's follow-through: _____

_____

Yesterday's act of self-care: _____

_____

What would make today great? _____

_____

I'm grateful for: _____

My top priority today: _____

What I'll do to support my top priority: _____

    ❑ **Step 1:** _____

    ❑ **Step 2:** _____

    ❑ **Step 3:** _____

Workday stopping time: _____

YOUR LITTLE CHALLENGE:

FORGIVE YOURSELF FOR SOMETHING IN THE PAST.

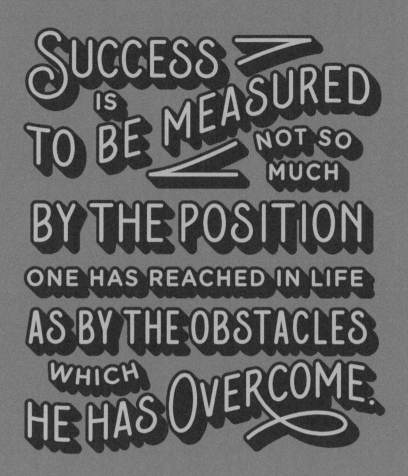

SUCCESS IS TO BE MEASURED NOT SO MUCH BY THE POSITION ONE HAS REACHED IN LIFE AS BY THE OBSTACLES WHICH HE HAS OVERCOME.

- BOOKER T. WASHINGTON

Vent/Rejoice/Plan/Note/List:

Date: _____ Time: _____ Location: _____

I feel: _____

Why I feel this way: _____

_____

_____

How'd it go yesterday? _____

_____

_____

Yesterday's productivity: _____

Today's follow-through: _____

_____

_____

Yesterday's act of self-care: _____

_____

_____

What would make today great? _____

_____

_____

I'm grateful for: _____

My top priority today: _____

What I'll do to support my top priority: _____

❑ **Step 1:** _____

❑ **Step 2:** _____

❑ **Step 3:** _____

Workday stopping time: _____

Vent/Rejoice/Plan/Note/List:

YOUR LITTLE CHALLENGE:

PAY SPECIAL ATTENTION TO YOUR PERSONAL GROOMING
TODAY—FOR NO OTHER REASON THAN BECAUSE
YOU'RE WORTH IT.

Date: _____ Time: _____ Location: _____

I feel: _____

Why I feel this way: _____

_____

_____

How'd it go yesterday? _____

_____

_____

Yesterday's productivity: _____

Today's follow-through: _____

_____

_____

Yesterday's act of self-care: _____

_____

_____

What would make today great? _____

_____

_____

I'm grateful for: _____

My top priority today: _____

What I'll do to support my top priority: _____

❑ **Step 1:** _____

❑ **Step 2:** _____

❑ **Step 3:** _____

Workday stopping time: _____

Vent/Rejoice/Plan/Note/List:

YOUR LITTLE CHALLENGE:

READ (OR REREAD) A BOOK ENTIRELY FOR PLEASURE.

Date: _____ Time: _____ Location: _____

I feel: _____

Why I feel this way: _____

_____

_____

How'd it go yesterday? _____

_____

_____

Yesterday's productivity: _____

Today's follow-through: _____

_____

_____

Yesterday's act of self-care: _____

_____

_____

What would make today great? _____

_____

_____

I'm grateful for: _____

My top priority today: _____

What I'll do to support my top priority: _____

❑ **Step 1:** _____

❑ **Step 2:** _____

❑ **Step 3:** _____

Workday stopping time: _____

Vent/Rejoice/Plan/Note/List:

YOUR LITTLE CHALLENGE:

STATE YOUR REAL (UNFILTERED) THOUGHTS ON A TOPIC.

Date: _____ Time: _____ Location: _____

I feel: _____

Why I feel this way: _____

_____

_____

How'd it go yesterday? _____

_____

_____

Yesterday's productivity: _____

Today's follow-through: _____

_____

_____

Yesterday's act of self-care: _____

_____

_____

What would make today great? _____

_____

_____

I'm grateful for: _____

My top priority today: _____

What I'll do to support my top priority: _____

    ❑ **Step 1:** _____

    ❑ **Step 2:** _____

    ❑ **Step 3:** _____

Workday stopping time: _____

Vent/Rejoice/Plan/Note/List:

_____

_____

_____

_____

_____

_____

_____

_____

_____

_____

_____

_____

_____

_____

_____

_____

_____

_____

_____

YOUR LITTLE CHALLENGE:

FORGIVE SOMEONE FOR A PAST WRONG.

Date: _____ Time: _____ Location: _____

I feel: _____

Why I feel this way: _____

_____

How'd it go yesterday? _____

_____

Yesterday's productivity: _____

Today's follow-through: _____

_____

Yesterday's act of self-care: _____

_____

What would make today great? _____

_____

I'm grateful for: _____

My top priority today: _____

What I'll do to support my top priority: _____

    ❑ **Step 1:** _____

    ❑ **Step 2:** _____

    ❑ **Step 3:** _____

Workday stopping time: _____

YOUR LITTLE CHALLENGE:

WHAT IS YOUR BEST QUALITY? WHY?
WRITE DOWN ALL THE REASONS.

IT IS NOT WORTHWHILE TO LET OUR IMPERFECTIONS DISTURB US ALWAYS.

- HENRY DAVID THOREAU

Vent/Rejoice/Plan/Note/List:

Date: _____ Time: _____ Location: _____

I feel: _____

Why I feel this way: _____

_____

_____

How'd it go yesterday? _____

_____

_____

Yesterday's productivity: _____

Today's follow-through: _____

_____

_____

Yesterday's act of self-care: _____

_____

_____

What would make today great? _____

_____

_____

I'm grateful for: _____

My top priority today: _____

What I'll do to support my top priority: _____

    ❑ **Step 1:** _____

    ❑ **Step 2:** _____

    ❑ **Step 3:** _____

Workday stopping time: _____

Vent/Rejoice/Plan/Note/List:

YOUR LITTLE CHALLENGE:

DRAW A PICTURE. SOAK IN THE WHOLE EXPERIENCE—THE COLORS, HOW THE LINES CONNECT, THE SIMPLE PLEASURE OF SEEING THE PICTURE TAKE SHAPE.

Date: _____ Time: _____ Location: _____

I feel: _____

Why I feel this way: _____

_____

_____

How'd it go yesterday? _____

_____

_____

Yesterday's productivity: _____

Today's follow-through: _____

_____

_____

Yesterday's act of self-care: _____

_____

_____

What would make today great? _____

_____

_____

I'm grateful for: _____

My top priority today: _____

What I'll do to support my top priority: _____

    ❑ **Step 1:** _____

    ❑ **Step 2:** _____

    ❑ **Step 3:** _____

Workday stopping time: _____

Vent/Rejoice/Plan/Note/List:

YOUR LITTLE CHALLENGE:

TAKE A TRIP TO SOMEWHERE YOU'VE NEVER BEEN.
(THIS COULD BE A LOCAL PLACE, A DAY TRIP,
OR A LONGER VACATION).

Date: _____ Time: _____ Location: _____

I feel: _____

Why I feel this way: _____

_____

_____

How'd it go yesterday? _____

_____

_____

Yesterday's productivity: _____

Today's follow-through: _____

_____

_____

Yesterday's act of self-care: _____

_____

_____

What would make today great? _____

_____

_____

I'm grateful for: _____

My top priority today: _____

What I'll do to support my top priority: _____

❑ **Step 1:** _____

❑ **Step 2:** _____

❑ **Step 3:** _____

Workday stopping time: _____

Vent/Rejoice/Plan/Note/List:

_____

_____

_____

_____

_____

_____

_____

_____

_____

_____

_____

_____

_____

_____

_____

_____

_____

_____

YOUR LITTLE CHALLENGE:

WRITE DOWN ONE THING THAT KEEPS YOU GOING. TAKE A MOMENT TO DO SO EACH DAY THIS WEEK.

Date: _____ Time: _____ Location: _____

I feel: _____

Why I feel this way: _____

_____

_____

How'd it go yesterday? _____

_____

_____

Yesterday's productivity: _____

Today's follow-through: _____

_____

_____

Yesterday's act of self-care: _____

_____

_____

What would make today great? _____

_____

_____

I'm grateful for: _____

My top priority today: _____

What I'll do to support my top priority: _____

    ❏ **Step 1:** _____

    ❏ **Step 2:** _____

    ❏ **Step 3:** _____

Workday stopping time: _____

Vent/Rejoice/Plan/Note/List:

YOUR LITTLE CHALLENGE:

LOOK IN THE MIRROR AND SMILE AT YOUR REFLECTION. REMIND YOURSELF THAT YOU'RE GREAT AND WORKING AT BECOMING BETTER EVERY DAY.

Date: _____ Time: _____ Location: _____

I feel: _____

Why I feel this way: _____

_____

How'd it go yesterday? _____

_____

Yesterday's productivity: _____

Today's follow-through: _____

_____

Yesterday's act of self-care: _____

_____

What would make today great? _____

_____

I'm grateful for: _____

My top priority today: _____

What I'll do to support my top priority: _____

    ❑ **Step 1:** _____

    ❑ **Step 2:** _____

    ❑ **Step 3:** _____

Workday stopping time: _____

YOUR LITTLE CHALLENGE:

TELL SOMEONE YOU LOVE THEM.

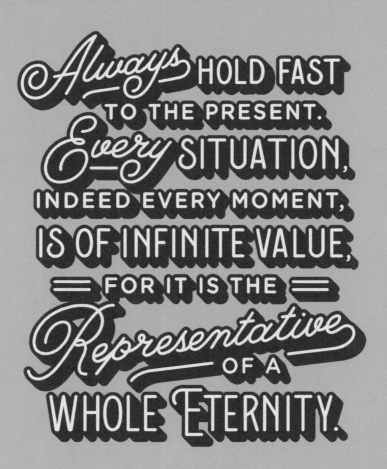

Always HOLD FAST TO THE PRESENT. Every SITUATION, INDEED EVERY MOMENT, IS OF INFINITE VALUE, FOR IT IS THE Representative OF A WHOLE ETERNITY.

- JOHANN WOLFGANG VON GOETHE

Vent/Rejoice/Plan/Note/List:

Date: _____ Time: _____ Location: _____

I feel: _____

Why I feel this way: _____

_____

How'd it go yesterday? _____

_____

Yesterday's productivity: _____

Today's follow-through: _____

_____

Yesterday's act of self-care: _____

_____

What would make today great? _____

_____

I'm grateful for: _____

My top priority today: _____

What I'll do to support my top priority: _____

❑ **Step 1:** _____

❑ **Step 2:** _____

❑ **Step 3:** _____

Workday stopping time: _____

YOUR LITTLE CHALLENGE:

ASK FOR SOMETHING YOU DON'T THINK YOU'LL GET. BE DARING!

SECURITY IS MOSTLY A *Superstition*. LIFE IS EITHER A *Daring* ADVENTURE — OR — NOTHING AT ALL.

- HELEN KELLER

Vent/Rejoice/Plan/Note/List:

Update Your Life Wheel

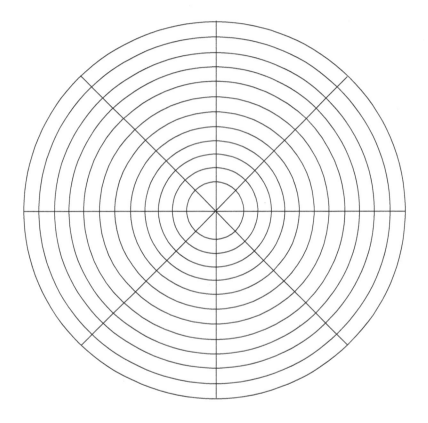

Date: _____ Time: _____ Location: _____

I feel: _____

Why I feel this way: _____

_____

_____

How'd it go yesterday? _____

_____

_____

Yesterday's productivity: _____

Today's follow-through: _____

_____

_____

Yesterday's act of self-care: _____

_____

_____

What would make today great? _____

_____

_____

I'm grateful for: _____

My top priority today: _____

What I'll do to support my top priority: _____

❑ **Step 1:** _____

❑ **Step 2:** _____

❑ **Step 3:** _____

Workday stopping time: _____

Vent/Rejoice/Plan/Note/List:

YOUR LITTLE CHALLENGE:

PRODUCE A SHORT AND SWEET TIMELINE FOR HOW
CHANGE IN YOUR LIFE HAS LED TO BETTER THINGS.

The Journal Entries   113

Date: _____ Time: _____ Location: _____

I feel: _____

Why I feel this way: _____

_____

_____

How'd it go yesterday? _____

_____

_____

Yesterday's productivity: _____

Today's follow-through: _____

_____

_____

Yesterday's act of self-care: _____

_____

_____

What would make today great? _____

_____

_____

I'm grateful for: _____

My top priority today: _____

What I'll do to support my top priority: _____

☐ **Step 1:** _____

☐ **Step 2:** _____

☐ **Step 3:** _____

Workday stopping time: _____

Vent/Rejoice/Plan/Note/List:

YOUR LITTLE CHALLENGE:

WHAT HAS BEEN YOUR GREATEST LIFE ACHIEVEMENT SO FAR? WRITE IT DOWN SO YOU CAN REVISIT IT WHENEVER YOU FEEL UNPRODUCTIVE.

Date: _____ Time: _____ Location: _____

I feel: _____

Why I feel this way: _____

_____

_____

How'd it go yesterday? _____

_____

_____

Yesterday's productivity: _____

Today's follow-through: _____

_____

_____

Yesterday's act of self-care: _____

_____

_____

What would make today great? _____

_____

_____

I'm grateful for: _____

My top priority today: _____

What I'll do to support my top priority: _____

❑ **Step 1:** _____

❑ **Step 2:** _____

❑ **Step 3:** _____

Workday stopping time: _____

Vent/Rejoice/Plan/Note/List:

_____

_____

_____

_____

_____

_____

_____

_____

_____

_____

_____

_____

_____

_____

_____

_____

_____

_____

YOUR LITTLE CHALLENGE:

BLOCK OFF AN HOUR OF YOUR TIME TO SPEND ALONE THIS WEEKEND—HOWEVER YOU WISH.

Date: _____ Time: _____ Location: _____

I feel: _____

Why I feel this way: _____

_____

_____

How'd it go yesterday? _____

_____

_____

Yesterday's productivity: _____

Today's follow-through: _____

_____

_____

Yesterday's act of self-care: _____

_____

_____

What would make today great? _____

_____

_____

I'm grateful for: _____

My top priority today: _____

What I'll do to support my top priority: _____

    ❑ **Step 1:** _____

    ❑ **Step 2:** _____

    ❑ **Step 3:** _____

Workday stopping time: _____

Vent/Rejoice/Plan/Note/List:

_____
_____
_____
_____
_____
_____
_____
_____
_____
_____
_____
_____
_____
_____
_____
_____
_____
_____
_____

YOUR LITTLE CHALLENGE:

TAKE A FOREIGN LANGUAGE CLASS AND TRY HAVING A SMALL CONVERSATION WITH SOMEONE WHO SPEAKS THAT LANGUAGE.

Date: _____ Time: _____ Location: _____

I feel: _____

Why I feel this way: _____

_____

How'd it go yesterday? _____

_____

Yesterday's productivity: _____

Today's follow-through: _____

_____

Yesterday's act of self-care: _____

_____

What would make today great? _____

_____

I'm grateful for: _____

My top priority today: _____

What I'll do to support my top priority: _____

❑ **Step 1:** _____

❑ **Step 2:** _____

❑ **Step 3:** _____

Workday stopping time: _____

YOUR LITTLE CHALLENGE:

RETRY A HOBBY THAT YOU'VE TRIED IN THE PAST THAT JUST DIDN'T STICK. SEE HOW THAT HOBBY MAKES YOU FEEL.

OUR GREATEST *Weakness* LIES IN GIVING UP. — THE MOST — CERTAIN WAY TO SUCCEED IS *Always* TO TRY JUST ONE MORE TIME.

- THOMAS EDISON

Vent/Rejoice/Plan/Note/List:

Date: _____ Time: _____ Location: _____

I feel: _____

Why I feel this way: _____

_____

_____

How'd it go yesterday? _____

_____

_____

Yesterday's productivity: _____

Today's follow-through: _____

_____

_____

Yesterday's act of self-care: _____

_____

_____

What would make today great? _____

_____

_____

I'm grateful for: _____

My top priority today: _____

What I'll do to support my top priority: _____

- ❏ **Step 1:** _____

- ❏ **Step 2:** _____

- ❏ **Step 3:** _____

Workday stopping time: _____

Vent/Rejoice/Plan/Note/List:

_____

_____

_____

_____

_____

_____

_____

_____

_____

_____

_____

_____

_____

_____

_____

_____

_____

_____

YOUR LITTLE CHALLENGE:

WRITE DOWN THE BIGGEST REASON YOU KNOW YOU'LL BE SUCCESSFUL AT REACHING YOUR NEXT GOAL.

Date: _____ Time: _____ Location: _____

I feel: _____

Why I feel this way: _____

_____

_____

How'd it go yesterday? _____

_____

_____

Yesterday's productivity: _____

Today's follow-through: _____

_____

_____

Yesterday's act of self-care: _____

_____

_____

What would make today great? _____

_____

_____

I'm grateful for: _____

My top priority today: _____

What I'll do to support my top priority: _____

    ❑ **Step 1:** _____

    ❑ **Step 2:** _____

    ❑ **Step 3:** _____

Workday stopping time: _____

Vent/Rejoice/Plan/Note/List:

YOUR LITTLE CHALLENGE:

MAKE A PLAYLIST OF YOUR FAVORITE SONGS AND PLAY IT
WHEN YOU'RE WORKING, CLEANING, EXERCISING,
OR IN THE SHOWER.

Date: _____ Time: _____ Location: _____

I feel: _____

Why I feel this way: _____

_____

_____

How'd it go yesterday? _____

_____

_____

Yesterday's productivity: _____

Today's follow-through: _____

_____

_____

Yesterday's act of self-care: _____

_____

_____

What would make today great? _____

_____

_____

I'm grateful for: _____

My top priority today: _____

What I'll do to support my top priority: _____

    ❑ **Step 1:** _____

    ❑ **Step 2:** _____

    ❑ **Step 3:** _____

Workday stopping time: _____

Vent/Rejoice/Plan/Note/List:

_____

_____

_____

_____

_____

_____

_____

_____

_____

_____

_____

_____

_____

_____

_____

_____

_____

_____

_____

_____

_____

YOUR LITTLE CHALLENGE:

DO A NEW SMALL THING YOU'VE NEVER DONE BEFORE AND PEPPER IT INTO YOUR DAILY ROUTINE FOR A WEEK. WRITE DOWN WHAT IT FELT LIKE TO SHAKE THINGS UP.

Date: _____ Time: _____ Location: _____

I feel: _____

Why I feel this way: _____

_____

_____

How'd it go yesterday? _____

_____

_____

Yesterday's productivity: _____

Today's follow-through: _____

_____

_____

Yesterday's act of self-care: _____

_____

_____

What would make today great? _____

_____

_____

I'm grateful for: _____

My top priority today: _____

What I'll do to support my top priority: _____

    ❑ **Step 1:** _____

    ❑ **Step 2:** _____

    ❑ **Step 3:** _____

Workday stopping time: _____

Vent/Rejoice/Plan/Note/List:

YOUR LITTLE CHALLENGE:

PICK ONE NEW HABIT YOU WANT TO CULTIVATE. TRACK IT
FOR 21 DAYS. HOW WAS YOUR CONSISTENCY?
CONGRATULATE YOURSELF FOR TRYING SOMETHING NEW.

Date: _____ Time: _____ Location: _____

I feel: _____

Why I feel this way: _____

_____

How'd it go yesterday? _____

_____

Yesterday's productivity: _____

Today's follow-through: _____

_____

Yesterday's act of self-care: _____

_____

What would make today great? _____

_____

I'm grateful for: _____

My top priority today: _____

What I'll do to support my top priority: _____

    ❑ **Step 1:** _____

    ❑ **Step 2:** _____

    ❑ **Step 3:** _____

Workday stopping time: _____

YOUR LITTLE CHALLENGE:

WRITE DOWN ONE WAY THAT WHAT YOU'RE DOING NOW MAKES THE WORLD A BETTER PLACE.

— WILLIAM JAMES

Vent/Rejoice/Plan/Note/List:

Date: _____ Time: _____ Location: _____

I feel: _____

Why I feel this way: _____

_____

_____

How'd it go yesterday? _____

_____

_____

Yesterday's productivity: _____

Today's follow-through: _____

_____

_____

Yesterday's act of self-care: _____

_____

_____

What would make today great? _____

_____

_____

I'm grateful for: _____

My top priority today: _____

What I'll do to support my top priority: _____

    ❑ **Step 1:** _____

    ❑ **Step 2:** _____

    ❑ **Step 3:** _____

Workday stopping time: _____

Vent/Rejoice/Plan/Note/List:

YOUR LITTLE CHALLENGE:

TAKE A NAP OR SLEEP IN.

Date: _____ Time: _____ Location: _____

I feel: _____

Why I feel this way: _____

_____

_____

How'd it go yesterday? _____

_____

_____

Yesterday's productivity: _____

Today's follow-through: _____

_____

_____

Yesterday's act of self-care: _____

_____

_____

What would make today great? _____

_____

_____

I'm grateful for: _____

My top priority today: _____

What I'll do to support my top priority: _____

    ❑ **Step 1:** _____

    ❑ **Step 2:** _____

    ❑ **Step 3:** _____

Workday stopping time: _____

Vent/Rejoice/Plan/Note/List:

YOUR LITTLE CHALLENGE:

TAKE ON A PHYSICAL CHALLENGE: A TWO-MILE JOG, 50 CRUNCHES, A DANCE CLASS— WHATEVER EXCITES YOU MOST.

The Journal Entries   135

Date: _____ Time: _____ Location: _____

I feel: _____

Why I feel this way: _____
_____
_____

How'd it go yesterday? _____
_____
_____

Yesterday's productivity: _____

Today's follow-through: _____
_____
_____

Yesterday's act of self-care: _____
_____
_____

What would make today great? _____
_____
_____

I'm grateful for: _____

My top priority today: _____

What I'll do to support my top priority: _____

   ❑ **Step 1:** _____

   ❑ **Step 2:** _____

   ❑ **Step 3:** _____

Workday stopping time: _____

Vent/Rejoice/Plan/Note/List:

YOUR LITTLE CHALLENGE:

RETRY A RECIPE THAT FLOPPED THE FIRST TIME YOU TRIED IT. DID THE DISH IMPROVE WITH REPEATED EFFORT?

Date: _____ Time: _____ Location: _____

I feel: _____

Why I feel this way: _____

_____

_____

How'd it go yesterday? _____

_____

_____

Yesterday's productivity: _____

Today's follow-through: _____

_____

_____

Yesterday's act of self-care: _____

_____

_____

What would make today great? _____

_____

_____

I'm grateful for: _____

My top priority today: _____

What I'll do to support my top priority: _____

    ❑ **Step 1:** _____

    ❑ **Step 2:** _____

    ❑ **Step 3:** _____

Workday stopping time: _____

Vent/Rejoice/Plan/Note/List:

YOUR LITTLE CHALLENGE:

LOOK AT SOMETHING THAT YOU'VE DONE AND ARE PROUD OF. ALLOW YOURSELF A MOMENT TO FEEL PRIDE IN YOUR ACCOMPLISHMENT.

Date: _____ Time: _____ Location: _____

I feel: _____

Why I feel this way: _____

_____

How'd it go yesterday? _____

_____

Yesterday's productivity: _____

Today's follow-through: _____

_____

Yesterday's act of self-care: _____

_____

What would make today great? _____

_____

I'm grateful for: _____

My top priority today: _____

What I'll do to support my top priority: _____

   ❑ **Step 1:** _____

   ❑ **Step 2:** _____

   ❑ **Step 3:** _____

Workday stopping time: _____

YOUR LITTLE CHALLENGE:

SPEND TIME WITH YOUR FAMILY/FRIENDS AND CONCENTRATE ON BEING FULLY PRESENT. ENJOY THE MOMENTS AS THEY COME.

THE BEST THING ABOUT THE *Future* IS THAT IT COMES ONLY ONE DAY AT A TIME.

- ABRAHAM LINCOLN

Vent/Rejoice/Plan/Note/List:

_____

_____

_____

_____

_____

_____

Date: _____ Time: _____ Location: _____

I feel: _____

Why I feel this way: _____

_____

How'd it go yesterday? _____

_____

Yesterday's productivity: _____

Today's follow-through: _____

_____

Yesterday's act of self-care: _____

_____

What would make today great? _____

_____

I'm grateful for: _____

My top priority today: _____

What I'll do to support my top priority: _____

❏ **Step 1:** _____

❏ **Step 2:** _____

❏ **Step 3:** _____

Workday stopping time: _____

YOUR LITTLE CHALLENGE:

DARE TO GO SOLO! GO OUT TO EAT, TO A MOVIE, SHOPPING, OR SOMETHING ELSE ALONE.

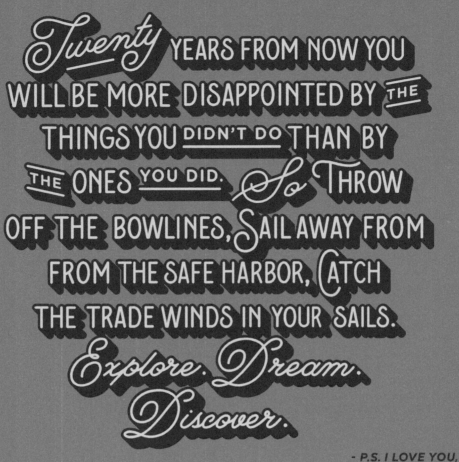

Twenty YEARS FROM NOW YOU WILL BE MORE DISAPPOINTED BY THE THINGS YOU DIDN'T DO THAN BY THE ONES YOU DID. So THROW OFF THE BOWLINES, Sail AWAY FROM FROM THE SAFE HARBOR, Catch THE TRADE WINDS IN YOUR SAILS. Explore. Dream. Discover.

- *P.S. I LOVE YOU,*
H. JACKSON BROWN

Vent/Rejoice/Plan/Note/List:

Date: _____ Time: _____ Location: _____

I feel: _____

Why I feel this way: _____

_____

_____

How'd it go yesterday? _____

_____

_____

Yesterday's productivity: _____

Today's follow-through: _____

_____

_____

Yesterday's act of self-care: _____

_____

_____

What would make today great? _____

_____

_____

I'm grateful for: _____

My top priority today: _____

What I'll do to support my top priority: _____

   ❏ **Step 1:** _____

   ❏ **Step 2:** _____

   ❏ **Step 3:** _____

Workday stopping time: _____

Vent/Rejoice/Plan/Note/List:

YOUR LITTLE CHALLENGE:

REMEMBER A TIME IN YOUR LIFE THAT WAS HARD BUT
DEFINED YOU OR MADE YOU GROW. WRITE DOWN THE
POSITIVES THAT CAME FROM THAT TIME.

Date: _____ Time: _____ Location: _____

I feel: _____

Why I feel this way: _____

_____

_____

How'd it go yesterday? _____

_____

_____

Yesterday's productivity: _____

Today's follow-through: _____

_____

_____

Yesterday's act of self-care: _____

_____

_____

What would make today great? _____

_____

_____

I'm grateful for: _____

My top priority today: _____

What I'll do to support my top priority: _____

   ❏ **Step 1:** _____

   ❏ **Step 2:** _____

   ❏ **Step 3:** _____

Workday stopping time: _____

Vent/Rejoice/Plan/Note/List:

YOUR LITTLE CHALLENGE:

GIVE BACK TO A CAUSE YOU BELIEVE IN. FOR ADDED
POINTS, ENCOURAGE OTHERS TO CONSIDER DONATING
AS WELL (TO WHATEVER CAUSE THEY DEEM IMPORTANT).

Date: _____ Time: _____ Location: _____

I feel: _____

Why I feel this way: _____

_____

_____

How'd it go yesterday? _____

_____

_____

Yesterday's productivity: _____

Today's follow-through: _____

_____

_____

Yesterday's act of self-care: _____

_____

_____

What would make today great? _____

_____

_____

I'm grateful for: _____

My top priority today: _____

What I'll do to support my top priority: _____

    ❑ **Step 1:** _____

    ❑ **Step 2:** _____

    ❑ **Step 3:** _____

Workday stopping time: _____

Vent/Rejoice/Plan/Note/List:

_____

_____

_____

_____

_____

_____

_____

_____

_____

_____

_____

_____

_____

_____

_____

_____

_____

_____

YOUR LITTLE CHALLENGE:

TAKE TIME TO SAVOR YOUR COFFEE/TEA THIS MORNING.

Date: _____ Time: _____ Location: _____

I feel: _____

Why I feel this way: _____

_____

_____

How'd it go yesterday? _____

_____

_____

Yesterday's productivity: _____

Today's follow-through: _____

_____

_____

_____

Yesterday's act of self-care: _____

_____

_____

What would make today great? _____

_____

_____

I'm grateful for: _____

My top priority today: _____

What I'll do to support my top priority: _____

   ❏ **Step 1:** _____

   ❏ **Step 2:** _____

   ❏ **Step 3:** _____

Workday stopping time: _____

Vent/Rejoice/Plan/Note/List:

YOUR LITTLE CHALLENGE:

TELL SOMEONE YOU APPRECIATE THEIR PRESENCE IN YOUR LIFE.

Date: _____ Time: _____ Location: _____

I feel: _____

Why I feel this way: _____

_____

How'd it go yesterday? _____

_____

Yesterday's productivity: _____

Today's follow-through: _____

_____

Yesterday's act of self-care: _____

_____

What would make today great? _____

_____

I'm grateful for: _____

My top priority today: _____

What I'll do to support my top priority: _____

□ **Step 1:** _____

□ **Step 2:** _____

□ **Step 3:** _____

Workday stopping time: _____

YOUR LITTLE CHALLENGE:

ASK FOR FEEDBACK FROM SOMEONE ABOUT HOW YOU CAN IMPROVE SOMETHING YOU'VE BEEN TRYING TO DO.

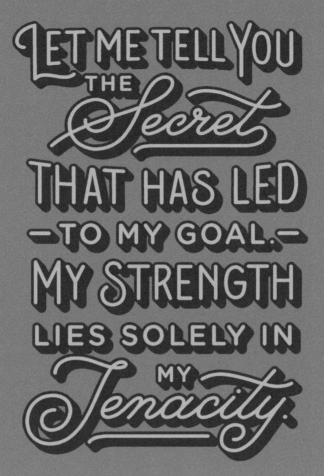

- LOUIS PASTEUR

Vent/Rejoice/Plan/Note/List:

Date: _____ Time: _____ Location: _____

I feel: _____

Why I feel this way: _____

_____

_____

How'd it go yesterday? _____

_____

_____

Yesterday's productivity: _____

Today's follow-through: _____

_____

_____

Yesterday's act of self-care: _____

_____

_____

What would make today great? _____

_____

_____

I'm grateful for: _____

My top priority today: _____

What I'll do to support my top priority: _____

    ❑ **Step 1:** _____

    ❑ **Step 2:** _____

    ❑ **Step 3:** _____

Workday stopping time: _____

Vent/Rejoice/Plan/Note/List:

YOUR LITTLE CHALLENGE:

DO SOMETHING GOOD FOR YOUR BODY—EAT A HEALTHY
MEAL, GO TO BED EARLY, NESSAGE YOUR NECK; ANYTHING
TO MAKE YOURSELF PHYSICALLY FEEL BETTER.

Date: _____ Time: _____ Location: _____

I feel: _____

Why I feel this way: _____

_____

_____

How'd it go yesterday? _____

_____

_____

Yesterday's productivity: _____

Today's follow-through: _____

_____

_____

Yesterday's act of self-care: _____

_____

_____

What would make today great? _____

_____

_____

I'm grateful for: _____

My top priority today: _____

What I'll do to support my top priority: _____

❑ **Step 1:** _____

❑ **Step 2:** _____

❑ **Step 3:** _____

Workday stopping time: _____

Vent/Rejoice/Plan/Note/List:

YOUR LITTLE CHALLENGE:

DECLUTTER OR CLEAN YOUR ENVIRONMENT (DOING SO IMPROVES YOUR MENTAL OUTLOOK AND HELPS YOU RELAX).

Date: _____ Time: _____ Location: _____

I feel: _____

Why I feel this way: _____

_____

_____

How'd it go yesterday? _____

_____

_____

Yesterday's productivity: _____

Today's follow-through: _____

_____

_____

Yesterday's act of self-care: _____

_____

_____

What would make today great? _____

_____

_____

I'm grateful for: _____

My top priority today: _____

What I'll do to support my top priority: _____

❑ **Step 1:** _____

❑ **Step 2:** _____

❑ **Step 3:** _____

Workday stopping time: _____

Vent/Rejoice/Plan/Note/List:

_____

_____

_____

_____

_____

_____

_____

_____

_____

_____

_____

_____

_____

_____

_____

_____

_____

_____

_____

_____

_____

YOUR LITTLE CHALLENGE:

GIVE SOMEONE YOU DON'T LIKE A (GOOD) GIFT OR DO SOMETHING NICE FOR THEM.

Update Your Life Wheel

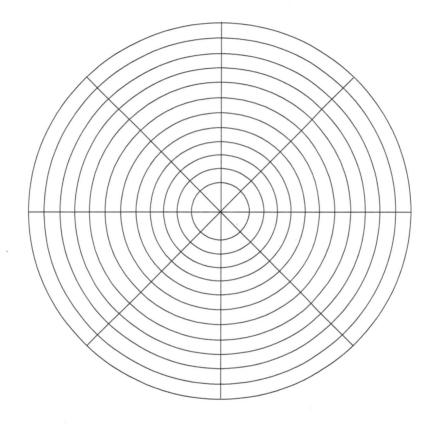

Date: _____ Time: _____ Location: _____

I feel: _____

Why I feel this way: _____

_____

_____

How'd it go yesterday? _____

_____

_____

Yesterday's productivity: _____

Today's follow-through: _____

_____

_____

Yesterday's act of self-care: _____

_____

_____

What would make today great? _____

_____

_____

I'm grateful for: _____

My top priority today: _____

What I'll do to support my top priority: _____

    ❑ **Step 1:** _____

    ❑ **Step 2:** _____

    ❑ **Step 3:** _____

Workday stopping time: _____

Vent/Rejoice/Plan/Note/List:

YOUR LITTLE CHALLENGE:

READ THE SUCCESS STORY OF SOMEONE YOU ADMIRE. WHAT WERE THEIR STRUGGLES LIKE? HOW CAN THEIR OBSTACLES RELATE TO YOURS?

Date: _____ Time: _____ Location: _____

I feel: _____

Why I feel this way: _____

_____

How'd it go yesterday? _____

_____

Yesterday's productivity: _____

Today's follow-through: _____

_____

Yesterday's act of self-care: _____

_____

What would make today great? _____

_____

I'm grateful for: _____

My top priority today: _____

What I'll do to support my top priority: _____

    ❑ **Step 1:** _____

    ❑ **Step 2:** _____

    ❑ **Step 3:** _____

Workday stopping time: _____

YOUR LITTLE CHALLENGE:

ALLOT YOURSELF A SMALL "FUN MONEY" BUDGET. SPEND IT ON SOMETHING JUST FOR YOU WITH NO GUILT.

- OSCAR WILDE

Vent/Rejoice/Plan/Note/List:

Date: _____ Time: _____ Location: _____

I feel: _____

Why I feel this way: _____

_____

_____

How'd it go yesterday? _____

_____

_____

Yesterday's productivity: _____

Today's follow-through: _____

_____

_____

Yesterday's act of self-care: _____

_____

_____

What would make today great? _____

_____

_____

I'm grateful for: _____

My top priority today: _____

What I'll do to support my top priority: _____

    ❏ **Step 1:** _____

    ❏ **Step 2:** _____

    ❏ **Step 3:** _____

Workday stopping time: _____

Vent/Rejoice/Plan/Note/List:

YOUR LITTLE CHALLENGE:

TAKE A LONG, WARM BATH.

Date: _____ Time: _____ Location: _____

I feel: _____

Why I feel this way: _____

_____

_____

How'd it go yesterday? _____

_____

_____

Yesterday's productivity: _____

Today's follow-through: _____

_____

_____

Yesterday's act of self-care: _____

_____

_____

What would make today great? _____

_____

_____

I'm grateful for: _____

My top priority today: _____

What I'll do to support my top priority: _____

- ❑ **Step 1:** _____

- ❑ **Step 2:** _____

- ❑ **Step 3:** _____

Workday stopping time: _____

Vent/Rejoice/Plan/Note/List:

_____

_____

_____

_____

_____

_____

_____

_____

_____

_____

_____

_____

_____

_____

_____

_____

_____

_____

YOUR LITTLE CHALLENGE:

TRY A CLASS YOU'VE NEVER TAKEN BEFORE (EXERCISE, DANCE, ART, ETC.).

Date: _____ Time: _____ Location: _____

I feel: _____

Why I feel this way: _____

_____

_____

How'd it go yesterday? _____

_____

_____

Yesterday's productivity: _____

Today's follow-through: _____

_____

_____

Yesterday's act of self-care: _____

_____

_____

What would make today great? _____

_____

_____

I'm grateful for: _____

My top priority today: _____

What I'll do to support my top priority: _____

❑ **Step 1:** _____

❑ **Step 2:** _____

❑ **Step 3:** _____

Workday stopping time: _____

Vent/Rejoice/Plan/Note/List:

_____
_____
_____
_____
_____
_____
_____
_____
_____
_____
_____
_____
_____
_____
_____
_____
_____
_____

YOUR LITTLE CHALLENGE:

THINK OF A SITUATION IN WHICH YOU OVERREACTED. REPLAY THAT SITUATION AS YOU WISH IT WOULD'VE HAPPENED. WRITE DOWN WHAT YOU CAN DO DIFFERENTLY IN SIMILAR FUTURE SITUATIONS.

Date: _____ Time: _____ Location: _____

I feel: _____

Why I feel this way: _____

_____

_____

How'd it go yesterday? _____

_____

_____

Yesterday's productivity: _____

Today's follow-through: _____

_____

_____

Yesterday's act of self-care: _____

_____

_____

What would make today great? _____

_____

_____

I'm grateful for: _____

My top priority today: _____

What I'll do to support my top priority: _____

   ❑ **Step 1:** _____

   ❑ **Step 2:** _____

   ❑ **Step 3:** _____

Workday stopping time: _____

Vent/Rejoice/Plan/Note/List:

YOUR LITTLE CHALLENGE:

WRITE DOWN GOOD QUALITIES ABOUT YOURSELF AND DESCRIPTIONS YOU WANT TO BE TRUE ABOUT YOURSELF. HIDE THEM (OR HAVE SOMEONE ELSE HIDE THEM) ALL OVER THE HOUSE FOR YOU TO FIND.

Date: _____ Time: _____ Location: _____

I feel: _____

Why I feel this way: _____
_____

How'd it go yesterday? _____
_____

Yesterday's productivity: _____

Today's follow-through: _____
_____

Yesterday's act of self-care: _____
_____

What would make today great? _____
_____

I'm grateful for: _____

My top priority today: _____

What I'll do to support my top priority:

❑ **Step 1:** _____

❑ **Step 2:** _____

❑ **Step 3:** _____

Workday stopping time: _____

YOUR LITTLE CHALLENGE:

SCHEDULE SOMETHING THAT MAKES YOU FEEL PAMPERED.

FOREVER — IS COMPOSED OF NOWS.

- EMILY DICKINSON

Vent/Rejoice/Plan/Note/List:

RESOURCES

Self-Discipline in 6 Weeks

This book helps you discover the joy of self-discipline and learn to be a goal catcher instead of just a goal setter. Even if you've failed at self-discipline in the past, this unique guide walks you through all the steps. You'll learn to address fears and come up with an actionable plan to help you channel the fire in your belly and cultivate creativity, resilience, mastering your time, and reaching your goals.

Questing for Self-Motivation to Achieve Your Personal Goals Course

Now that you have the self-discipline to set your goals and achieve the life of your dreams, it's time to work on the motivation to get started. Oftentimes, starting is the hardest part. Just like self-discipline, self-motivation is a set of skills you can learn. This course features a workable system with video lessons, slides, and worksheets you can apply to any personal goal. Get the motivation to both chase and catch your dreams and personal goals today! SubscribePage.com/Questing-For-Self-Motivation-Course

The Pearl Perspective

We all experience self-doubt from time to time. It's hard to set and pursue goals when you're besieged by your inner critic, worrying too much, and don't feel like you have a support group. This uplifting book is the personal development starting point I wish I had at the beginning of my journey. It's full of relatable confessions and examples, covering topics such as mindfulness, gratitude, worry, self-comparison, self-talk, learning from hard times in our lives, setting goals, making choices, handling critics and criticism, and building your support network.
https://www.SubscribePage.com/PearlPerspective

Contentment Questing

Contentment Questing is my personal development website, designed to help cultivate a life you love and manage your time productively. Enter your email address for access to my VIP Library with helpful and supportive printables. As a bonus, you get weekly words of encouragement from me and priority email access. Let me personally help you manage your time, be productive, and find the joy in your life.

ContentmentQuesting.com

REFERENCES

Tervooren, Tyler. "27 Simple Tactics You Can Use Today to Become an Intrepid Risk-Taker." Riskology. Accessed May 5, 2020. Riskology.co/27-simple-tactics-you-can-use-today-to-become-an-intrepid-risk-taker.

Tracy, Brian. *Eat That Frog! 21 Great Ways to Stop Procrastinating and Get More Done in Less Time.* Oakland: Berrett-Koehler Publishers, Inc., 2017.

Webb, Jennifer. *Self-Discipline in 6 Weeks.* Emeryville: Rockridge Press, 2020.

ACKNOWLEDGMENTS

I would like to thank my editor, Tasha, for her hard work on this book. I would also like to thank Callisto Media for this opportunity to share my writing and make my own impact on the world.

Most of all, I would like to thank my Lord and Savior, Jesus Christ. Without Him, none of this would be possible. He uplifts me and gives me strength and hope through the hardest times in my life. He is my rock and the anchor of my soul. If I've been able to say anything to uplift you, reader, in the course of this book, give Him the honor for it.

ABOUT THE AUTHOR

 **Jennifer Webb** is an author and personal development blogger. You can see more from her on her blog at ContentmentQuesting.com, where she's committed to helping people find the joy in their lives, even through hard times. Her other books include *Self-Discipline in 6 Weeks: How to Set Goals with Soul and Make Your Habits Work for You* and *The Pearl Perspective: How Changing Your Perspective Can Change Your Life*. She also has an online course, Self-Motivation Strategies to Achieve Your Personal Goals, designed to give you the inner drive you've always wanted injust 15 minutes a day for one week. She lives in a small community in Arkansas, with her husband, Shanon, and their two sons. She enjoys blogging, reading, horse-back riding, hiking, camping, traveling, and spending time with her family and friends. She would love to hear your personal success story! You can email her at jennifer@contentmentquesting.com

CPSIA information can be obtained
at www.ICGtesting.com
Printed in the USA
JSHW011949060521
14409JS00002B/2

9 781647 398545